FANTASTIC BEASTS
AND WHERE TO FIND THEM™

NEWT SCAMANDER™

CINEMATIC GUIDE

J.K. ROWLING'S WIZARDING WORLD

SCHOLASTIC LTD.

www.fantasticbeasts.co.uk

Scholastic Children's Books
Euston House, 24 Eversholt Street,
London NW1 1DB, UK

A division of Scholastic Ltd
London ~ New York ~ Toronto ~ Sydney ~ Auckland
Mexico City ~ New Delhi ~ Hong Kong

First published in the US by Scholastic Inc, 2017
Published in the UK by Scholastic Ltd, 2017

By Felicity Baker
Art Direction: Rick DeMonico
Page Design: Heather Barber

ISBN 978 1407 17940 7

Printed in the UK by Bell and Bain Ltd, Glasgow

2 4 6 8 10 9 7 5 3 1

www.scholastic.co.uk

CONTENTS

FILM BEGINNINGS

In 1926, a wizard named Newt Scamander arrives in the United States of America. Wizards and witches live entirely in secret here, which means Newt must blend in with the Muggles – or what American wizards call 'No-Majs'. But appearing ordinary will prove difficult for the eccentric Newt, especially when his case full of fantastic beasts is accidentally opened!

Newton Artemis Fido Scamander –
nicknamed 'Newt' – is from a well-established,
English wizarding family.

He was taught at Hogwarts School of Witchcraft and Wizardry, where he took great interest in the Care of Magical Creatures class. While a student, he was sorted into Hufflepuff house.

Albus Dumbledore, the Transfiguration professor at Hogwarts, thought highly of his pupil, Newt Scamander.

When the Great War erupted, Newt served his country in a confidential programme for the Ministry of Magic's Beast Division.

Newt's primary charge was handling dragons, particularly Ukrainian Ironbellies, on the Eastern Front. The programme failed because the dragons would only respond to him and tried to eat everyone else.

"I'VE JUST COMPLETED A YEAR IN THE FIELD. I'M WRITING A BOOK ABOUT MAGICAL CREATURES... A GUIDE TO HELP PEOPLE UNDERSTAND WHY WE SHOULD BE PROTECTING THESE CREATURES INSTEAD OF KILLING THEM."

-NEWT SCAMANDER

Newt spent his years after the war travelling the world, from Sudan to Equatorial Guinea, to do research for his book titled *Fantastic Beasts and Where to Find Them.*

Newt's wizarding skills extend beyond the training of creatures.

Since he has journeyed far and wide through remote and dangerous locations, Newt has had to learn how to cast a wide range of spells.

Newt casts the spell 'Alohomora!' to open the vault at a bank in New York City. He's not there to steal gold, but to nab his escaped Niffler.

The Niffler is a small creature with an insatiable appetite for shiny things.

Newt moves around quickly using the magical transportation mode known as 'Apparation'. It makes him disappear from one location and reappear in another place of his choice. Someone who is in physical contact with him at the time can also disappear and reappear with him.

An Occamy egg rolls out of Newt's case at a bank. Jacob Kowalski, a No-Maj, picks it up just in time to feel it rumbling before it hatches. Newt quickly Apparates outside the bank with Jacob so he does not draw attention to them.

There are times when No-Majs witness feats of wizardry they shouldn't see. Standard practice is to 'Obliviate' portions of their memories and make them forget what they have seen. However, Newt does not cast this spell on Jacob Kowalski, the No-Maj he befriends.

When the police arrive in New York City's Diamond District to check out a break-in, they discover Newt and Jacob at the scene of the crime. Once again, Newt quickly Apparates with Jacob to get away!

When Newt pursues something, he doesn't give up easily. He's always looking for the truth, particularly involving legendary creatures. He will go to the ends of the earth if necessary.

JACOB: "SO WHAT, YOU— YOU RESCUE THESE CREATURES?"

NEWT: "YES, THAT'S RIGHT. RESCUE, NURTURE AND PROTECT THEM, AND I'M GENTLY TRYING TO EDUCATE MY FELLOW WIZARDS ABOUT THEM."

Beasts don't frighten Newt – what scares him are witches and wizards who think *all* magical creatures are dangerous and should be feared or exterminated.

COMING TO AMERICA

Newt arrives in New York City on a steamship, carrying a case filled with all sorts of magical creatures. But all is not right in the city. Some mysterious force is causing untold damage, frightening witches, wizards and No-Majs alike.

Newt has to have his passport checked and his case inspected to satisfy the United States customs official.

Newt quickly turns the lock on his case to the 'Muggle Worthy'
setting. Now the customs official is only able to see Newt's ordinary
personal belongings – not his collection of magical beasts!

CUSTOMS OFFICIAL: "BRITISH, HUH?"

NEWT: "YES."

CUSTOMS OFFICIAL: "FIRST TRIP TO NEW YORK?"

NEWT: "YES."

CUSTOMS OFFICIAL: "ANYTHING EDIBLE IN THERE?"

NEWT: "NO."

After clearing customs, Newt discovers that witches and wizards live in hiding in America.

Newt joins a crowd gathered around Mary Lou Barebone, the leader of the New Salem Philanthropic Society.

A young woman named Tina Goldstein lurks in the crowd eating a hot dog. She's as much of an outsider in this crowd as Newt is – she's a witch!

Mary Lou Barebone believes witches and wizards live among them. She blames witches and wizards for causing the destruction that is tearing the whole city apart.

"SOMETHING IS STALKING OUR CITY, WREAKING DESTRUCTION, THEN VANISHING WITHOUT A TRACE."

—MARY LOU BAREBONE

Newt's case has more than just his long johns inside!

While Newt listens to Mary Lou's speech, a Niffler crawls out of his case.

Newt follows the little creature into a bank.

The bank is where Newt first encounters the No-Maj, Jacob Kowalski. He currently works in a canning factory and needs a loan to open his own bakery.

In the bank, Jacob witnesses Newt casting spells in an attempt to catch the Niffler. Before Newt can Obliviate Jacob, the No-Maj escapes – and inadvertently takes Newt's case!

Tina scolds Newt for using magic in front of No-Majs and for not Obliviating Jacob.

Tina takes Newt to MACUSA – the Magical Congress of the United States of America – for questioning.

MACUSA headquarters is located inside the Woolworth Building
on Broadway.

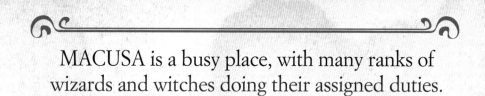

MACUSA is a busy place, with many ranks of wizards and witches doing their assigned duties.

Tina takes Newt into the Major Investigation Department and interrupts a discussion between President Seraphina Picquery and Percival Graves, the Director of Magical Security, concerning the mysterious attacks in New York.

Down in the basement, Tina explains that all foreigners have to hold a wand permit in New York.

Suspicious of why Newt came to New York, Graves goes down to the basement to talk to him. Graves looks inside Newt's case to find... Polish pastries. The truth is revealed. Jacob has Newt's creature-filled case!

The search for his case sends Newt on a wild chase across New York City.

With Tina in tow, Newt heads to a Lower East Side neighbourhood to find Jacob and reclaim his case.

Newt enters Jacob's apartment first and sees him lying on the floor, nearly unconscious. The apartment is in a shambles and an entire wall has been smashed. Before Tina can see the mess and reprimand Newt, he quickly casts the Repairing Charm to set things right.

Newt and Tina quickly realize what caused the chaos – his case has been opened and some of the beasts have escaped – including a very powerful one, the Erumpent, that ploughed through the brick wall! Newt also recognizes that the bite on Jacob's neck is from a Murtlap.

Tina lives with her sister, Queenie.

Queenie prepares a delicious supper for their guests, but Newt's thoughts are on his beasts.

Jacob recuperates in the girls' bedroom while sipping on a hot drink.

Newt doesn't go to sleep immediately. He opens his case and descends into it, motioning for Jacob to follow him down.

Newt gets a grand tour of the city while pursuing his beasts.

Hunting for the Niffler takes Newt and Jacob into the city's Diamond District, which has all sorts of shiny jewellery for sale.

Newt and Jacob also make a night-time visit to the Central Park Zoo to try to catch the stampeding Erumpent.

The Goldstein sisters take Newt and Jacob to a wizarding speakeasy, The Blind Pig. Gnarlak, the Goblin owner, may possess information that will help Newt.

FRIENDS AND FOES

A loner by nature, Newt doesn't have many close relationships with people. He prefers to spend his time interacting with magical creatures. But while in New York, he does make some human friends – and some enemies.

Tina Goldstein was once an Auror for MACUSA investigating magical crimes. Though she has been demoted, she still gets upset when Newt Scamander flouts the rules.

Over the course of recapturing Newt's creatures, Tina learns that the motivations of the law-breaking wizard are good and genuine, unlike some leaders at MACUSA. They begin to develop feelings for each other.

"IF I DON'T COME BACK, LOOK AFTER MY CREATURES. EVERYTHING THAT YOU NEED TO KNOW IS IN THERE."

–NEWT SCAMANDER TO TINA GOLDSTEIN,
ON HIS MANUSCRIPT

Queenie has perfected the wizarding skill of Legilimency, which allows one to read another's mind.

She hears her sister's mental cry for help and rushes to MACUSA headquarters to rescue Tina.

When Jacob Kowalski bumps into
Newt Scamander, he enters a world he never
knew existed.

Jacob realizes that whatever is moving inside his case isn't one
of his pastries.

"THIS IS ALL JUST SOME BIG NIGHTMARE, RIGHT?"

—JACOB KOWALSKI

At first, Newt's fantastic beasts frighten Jacob, but over time he learns to accept them. Still, he must wear protective gear when confronting a large creature like the Erumpent.

JACOB: **"WHY— WHY WOULD I HAVE TO WEAR SOMETHING LIKE THIS?"**

NEWT: **"BECAUSE YOUR SKULL IS SUSCEPTIBLE TO BREAKAGE UNDER IMMENSE FORCE."**

He might be 'just' a No-Maj, but Jacob proves himself to be very helpful in the search for Newt's beasts.

The Magical Congress of the United States of America thinks Newt Scamander and his fantastic beasts are a danger to the city.

When Newt warns MACUSA President Seraphina Picquery that the attacks are being caused by a deadly creature called an Obscurus, she rebuffs his claim and orders Newt and his friends to be reprimanded.

"YOU ARE AN INTERESTING MAN, MR SCAMANDER."

-PERCIVAL GRAVES

Graves believes Newt released the beasts to incite a war between No-Majs and wizards.

MAGIZOOLOGY

Newt is a Magizoologist – someone who
studies and cares for magical creatures.

Newt's case looks like any ordinary leather case on the outside, but inside it contains a magical world of its own.

The world inside Newt's case contains many specialized biomes – habitats for his beasts. Newt has created them to meet the needs of the various creatures that inhabit them. He stores crates of food and keeps charts on the beasts' feeding requirements.

SPECIAL FEED CODES

	Beaked (excl. Griffin)	
	Feathered	
	Horned	
	Hooved (not Nogtails)	
	Carapaced	

HABITAT & TERRAIN CODES

	Aquatic / Amphibious	
	Burrowing	
	Desert	
	Tropical / Equatorial	
	Temperate	

FANTASTIC BEASTS
AND WHERE TO FIND THEM

Newt has built a perfect habitat for himself, too. His shed is packed from floor to ceiling with fascinating artefacts and tools he uses in his world travels.

Newt writes his manuscript about fantastic creatures in his shed.

While in the shed, Newt mixes salves and potions, like the one he makes for Jacob to heal his Murtlap bite.

Newt invites Jacob inside his case and shows him how marvellous
magical creatures are.

"I WANT TO BE A WIZARD."

-JACOB KOWALSKI

FANTASTIC BEASTS

The wizarding world has a multitude of diverse creatures and magical species. Many of these fantastic creatures were deemed forever lost, until Newt Scamander trekked to unknown areas, found them and rescued them from possible extinction.

Niffler

The Niffler looks like a black furry mole with a pointy snout. Its beady eyes are always searching for shiny things like keys, coins and even dental fillings! Once such an object is found, the Niffler won't stop until that object is in its magically extending belly-pouch.

"FOR THE LAST TIME, YOU PILFERING PEST – PAWS OFF WHAT DOESN'T BELONG TO YOU!"

–NEWT SCAMANDER TO HIS NIFFLER

Murtlap

The Murtlap is a fierce creature that is known for its vicious bite. Tentacles grow on the back of its rodent body and they wiggle aggressively when the creature is provoked.

For No-Majs like Jacob Kowalski, a Murtlap bite will make them itchy, twitchy and ill – and might even cause flames to shoot out from their behinds! When pickled and eaten, Murtlap growths can give immunity to curses and jinxes.

Thunderbird

The Thunderbird is one of the most majestic creatures ever to exist. When it senses danger, it flaps its six massive wings, creating a torrential thunderstorm. Newt rescued a Thunderbird he named Frank from a group of poachers. He has come to the United States to return Frank to his natural habitat, the desert of the south-west.

"HE'S A WEE BIT SENSITIVE TO STRANGERS."

-NEWT ON FRANK THE THUNDERBIRD

Swooping Evil

A beautiful but deadly creature, the Swooping Evil has magnificent wings like those of a butterfly, yet long, sharp fangs and the scaly body of a reptile. The creature got its name from locals who said it sucked out the brains of humans. When at rest, the Swooping Evil folds into a small, spiny cocoon that contains sparkling venom. Newt suspects that if properly diluted, this venom can remove unpleasant memories.

Bowtruckle

It can be hard to spot a Bowtruckle in a tree because its body resembles stems and leaves. These tiny creatures are energetic and chatty, though some can suffer from bouts of separation anxiety.

Titus, Finn and Poppy are some of the Bowtruckles that inhabit the bamboo forest in Newt's case. The shyest of the bunch, Pickett, has found a happy home in the pocket of Newt's greatcoat. Pickett helps Newt out by using his thin fingers to pick locks.

"HE'S HAD A COLD. HE NEEDED SOME BODY WARMTH."

-NEWT SCAMANDER ON PICKETT

Billywig

The Billywig is an insect with a sapphire blue body and glittering wings. It's a fast flyer, which helps it zip from place to place.

Tina sees one of Newt's beasts, a Billywig, flying above a crowd of New Yorkers. Several people nearby see the creature as well.

Mooncalf

Newt's herd of Mooncalves live on a moonlit rock face. These sheepish, giant-eyed creatures have smooth skin and webbed feet. They're skittish when it comes to people they don't know, but Jacob wins them over by feeding them food pellets. In turn, their tenderness soothes his own fears of the magical world.

Occamy

This rare, winged reptile has a bounty
of shimmering scales and vibrant purple
feathers that astound anyone who sees it.
Perhaps even more amazing is that the Occamy
is 'choranaptyxic', meaning it has the ability
to modify its body in size and shape.

"THEY LEARN TO DEFEND THEMSELVES EARLY. SEE, THEIR SHELLS ARE MADE OF SILVER, SO THEY'RE INCREDIBLY VALUABLE."

-NEWT SCAMANDER ON THE OCCAMY

Newt tricks the Occamy that escaped from his case by dropping a cockroach into a teapot. Tina holds the teapot out and the Occamy shrinks itself to fit inside to reach the tasty snack.

Erumpent

Many feet taller than an elephant, the Erumpent has a thick, armoured hide and a horn like a rhinoceros. It is usually peaceful, except during mating season when females can go on furious stampedes in search of a mate. Its sharp horn contains a lethal fluid that will cause whatever it pierces to explode.

Demiguise

The Demiguise is a wise, apelike creature with silky, white fur. These small beasts have the power to become invisible. They're also imbued with a keen sense of precognition, allowing them to predict what others will do before they actually do it. While the creature is seeing the future, its eyes glow.

The Demiguise's abilities make it an incredibly challenging creature to capture. Only by being completely unpredictable can one manage to outwit this creature, as Newt does with a Demiguise he calls Dougal.

The Obscurus

An Obscurus has not been seen in the United States for 200 years. It is a chaotic entity of incredible, violent energy. Newt has contained one inside his case for further study.

"THERE'S NO DOCUMENTED CASE OF ANY OBSCURIAL SURVIVING PAST THE AGE OF TEN. THE ONE I MET IN AFRICA WAS EIGHT WHEN SHE— SHE WAS EIGHT, WHEN SHE DIED."

-NEWT SCAMANDER

An Obscurus comes into existence when a child represses his or her magical talent. It brews like a storm inside the child, until it erupts into the world, causing destruction wherever it goes. The power of the Obscurus frequently kills its host child before the age of ten.

"I'VE CHANGED. I THINK. MAYBE A LITTLE."

-NEWT SCAMANDER